DATE DUE	
SEP 2 2 2012		
NOV 01 2012	FEB 1 1 2013	
MAR 1 9 2013		

The Urbana Free Library

To renew: call 217-367-4057
or go to "*urbanafreelibrary.org*"
and select "Renew/Request Items"

A LITTLE JAMIE BOOK

What It's Like to Be
Qué se siente al ser

PRESIDENT

BARACK OBAMA

BY/POR PATRICE SHERMAN

TRANSLATED BY/TRADUCIDO
POR
EIDA DE LA VEGA

Mitchell Lane

PUBLISHERS

P.O. Box 196
Hockessin, Delaware 19707
Visit us on the web: www.mitchelllane.com
Comments? email us:
mitchelllane@mitchelllane.com

8/10
25%

Mitchell Lane
PUBLISHERS

Printing   2   3   4   5   6   7   8   9

LITTLE JAMIE BOOKS

What It's Like to Be . . .   Qué se siente al ser . . .

America Ferrera/América Ferrera
The Jonas Brothers/Los Hermanos Jonas
Marta Vieira
Miley Cyrus
President Barack Obama/El Presidente Barack Obama
Ryan Howard
Shakira
Sonia Sotomayor

Library of Congress Cataloging-in-Publication Data
Sherman, Patrice.
  What it's like to be president Barack Obama? / by Patrice Sherman; translated by Eida de la Vega = ¿Qué se siente al ser el presidente Barack Obama? / por Patrice Sherman; traducido por Eida de la Vega.
    p. cm — A little Jamie book = Un libro little Jaime)
  Includes bibliographical references and index.
  ISBN 978-1-58415-843-1 (library bound)
  1. Obama, Barack — Juvenile literature. 2. Presidents — United States — Biography — Juvenile literature. I. Vega, Eida de la. II. Title. III. Title: ¿Qué se siente al ser el presidente Barack Obama?
  E908.S54 2010
  973.932092 — dc22
  [B]

                                                                                    20090292

ABOUT THE AUTHOR: Children's book writer Patrice Sherman lives in Cambridge, Massachusetts, not far from Harvard University where Barack Obama attended law school. She enjoys reading about history and also likes to visit the John F. Kennedy Presidential Library and Museum in nearby Boston.

ACERCA DE LOS AUTORES: Pat Sherman vive y escribe en Cambridge, Massachusetts, cerca de la ciudad de Boston. Es aficionada a los Medias Rojas, pero cuando visita a su hermana en Pensilvania, le gusta apoyar a los Filis.

ABOUT THE TRANSLATOR: Eida de la Vega was born in Havana, Cuba, and now lives in New Jersey with her mother, her husband, and her two children. Eida has worked at Lectorum/Scholastic, and as editor of the magazine *Selecciones del Reader's Digest*.

ACERCA DE LA TRADUCTORA: Eida de la Vega nació en La Habana, Cuba, y ahora vive en Nueva Jersey con su madre, su esposo y sus dos hijos. Ha trabajado en Lectorum/Scholastic y, como editora, en la revista *Selecciones del Reader's Digest*.

PLB / PLB2

What It's Like to Be/
Qué se siente al ser el presidente

PRESIDENT BARACK OBAMA

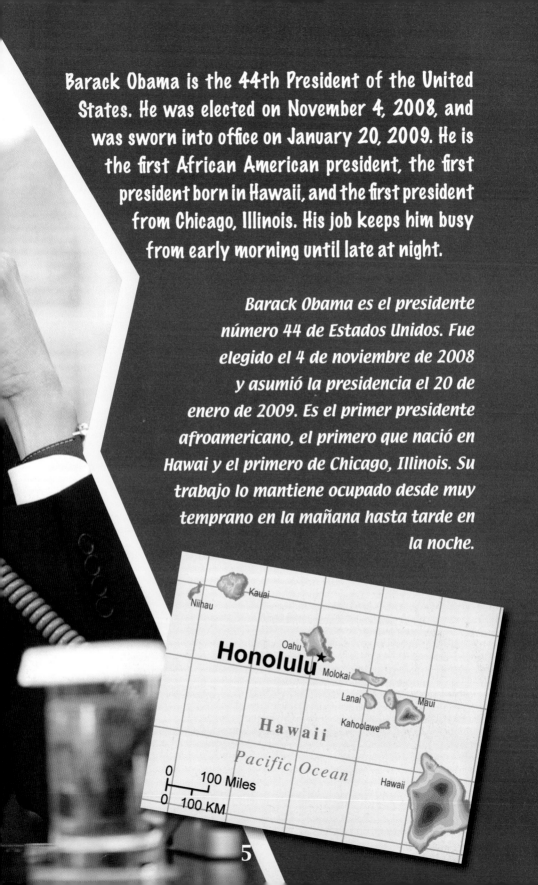

Barack Obama is the 44th President of the United States. He was elected on November 4, 2008, and was sworn into office on January 20, 2009. He is the first African American president, the first president born in Hawaii, and the first president from Chicago, Illinois. His job keeps him busy from early morning until late at night.

Barack Obama es el presidente número 44 de Estados Unidos. Fue elegido el 4 de noviembre de 2008 y asumió la presidencia el 20 de enero de 2009. Es el primer presidente afroamericano, el primero que nació en Hawai y el primero de Chicago, Illinois. Su trabajo lo mantiene ocupado desde muy temprano en la mañana hasta tarde en la noche.

President Obama lives with his wife, Michelle, and their daughters, Malia and Sasha, in the White House at 1600 Pennsylvania Avenue in Washington, D.C. Every morning, he says good-bye to Malia and Sasha before they go to school. Then he rides the elevator downstairs to work. He begins at the Oval Office to talk with his staff.

El presidente Obama vive con su esposa, Michelle, y sus hijas, Malia y Sasha, en la Casa Blanca, situada en el número 1600 de la avenida Pensilvania, en Washington D.C. Por la mañana, despide a Malia y a Sasha cuando se van a la escuela. Luego, baja en el elevador para ir a trabajar. Lo primero que hace es reunirse con sus asesores en el Despacho Oval.

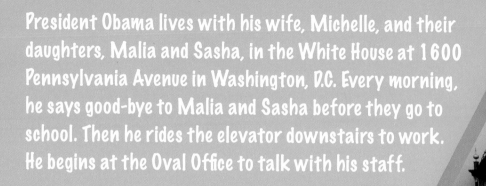

FIRST FAMILY (LA FAMILIA DEL PRESIDENTE)

APPLES
(MANZANAS)

7

After his staff updates him on the most important issues of the day, Obama goes to his morning press conference. Reporters ask him a lot of questions about current events and his plans for the nation's future.

Despues de que sus asesores lo actualizan sobre los temas más importantes del día, Obama se dirige a su rueda de prensa matinal. Los periodistas le hacen montones de preguntas acerca de acontecimientos actuales y de sus planes para el futuro de la nación.

MICROPHONE

QUILL PEN AND INK
(PLUMA DE AVE PARA
ESCRIBIR Y TINTA)

After the press conference, he goes back to his office to sign important bills and acts into law. Every law passed by Congress needs to be signed by the president. Sometimes he gives the pen he used to one of the people who helped create the bill.

Después de que termina la rueda de prensa, vuelve a su despacho para firmar proyectos de leyes y actas con el fin de convertirlos en leyes. Todas las leyes aprobadas por el Congreso tienen que ser firmadas por el Presidente. En ocasiones, el Presidente le regala la pluma con la que firmó la ley a una de las personas que ayudó a crear el proyecto de ley.

President Obama takes a break to play golf with Vice President Joe Biden on the White House lawn. Sometimes he'll shoot hoops on an indoor basketball court.

El presidente Obama toma un receso para jugar golf con el vicepresidente Joe Biden en el césped de la Casa Blanca. A veces, le tira al aro en una cancha de baloncesto bajo techo.

The President usually holds meetings over lunch. He may eat in the White House, or he'll slip out with Vice President Biden for a bite at a local restaurant. He eats a lot of healthy fruits and vegetables, but often makes room for his favorite—a burger and fries.

El Presidente celebra reuniones mientras almuerza. Puede comer en la Casa Blanca o darse una escapadita con el vicepresidente Biden a un restaurante cercano. Come muchas frutas y verduras saludables, pero con frecuencia deja un espacio para su comida favorita: hamburguesa y papas fritas.

CHEESE, CRACKERS AND CARROTS (QUESO, GALLETAS Y ZANAHORIAS)

In the afternoon, he meets with his Cabinet. The men and women of the Cabinet are the heads of the main government departments, including the Departments of Agriculture, Defense, Education, and Transportation. They give the president advice and help carry out his policies.

Por la tarde, se reúne con su gabinete. Los hombres y mujeres de su gabinete son quienes dirigen los principales departamentos del gobierno, incluyendo el Departamento de Agricultura, de Defensa, de Educación y de Transporte. Le dan consejos al Presidente y lo ayudan a llevar a cabo sus proyectos políticos.

BO, THE FIRST DOG
(BO, LA PERRITA DE
LOS OBAMA)

When Malia and Sasha come home, their dad helps them take their Portuguese Water Dog, Bo, for a walk. The girls tell the President what they did in school that day.

Cuando Malia y Sasha regresan a casa, su papá las ayuda a sacar a pasear a Bo, su perra de aguas portuguesa. Las niñas le cuentan al Presidente lo que hicieron en la escuela ese día.

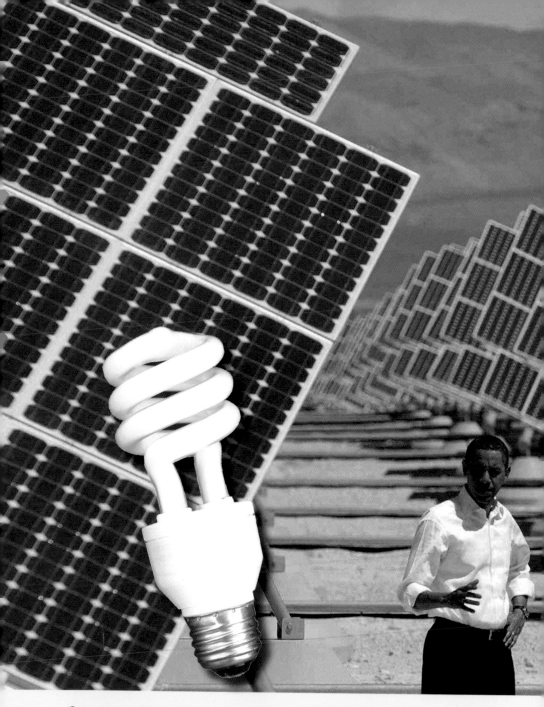

President Obama often leaves the White House to talk to people. He encourages Americans to develop new sources of energy. In early 2009, he toured a field of solar panels at Nellis Air Force Base in Nevada.

El presidente Obama sale con frecuencia de la Casa Blanca para hablar con la gente. Anima a los estadounidenses a desarrollar nuevas fuentes de energía. A principios de 2009, visitó un campo de paneles solares en la Base de la Fuerza Aérea Nellis, en Nevada.

The President holds town hall meetings throughout the country. These meetings give people a chance to ask questions and to tell him what they think about important issues. He tries to make the best decisions possible based on everything he hears.

El Presidente celebra reuniones en alcaldías de todo el país.
Estas reuniones le ofrecen a la gente la oportunidad de
hacer preguntas y de decirle al Presidente lo que piensan
sobre asuntos importantes. Él trata de tomar las mejores
decisiones posibles en dependencia de lo que oye.

Back at the White House, many famous people are invited to visit the President, including the 2008 World Series champions, the Philadelphia Phillies.

PRESIDENT OBAMA

24

Muchas personas son invitadas a la Casa Blanca a visitar al Presidente, como los campeones de la Serie Mundial de Béisbol 2008, los Filis de Filadelfia.

In the evening, family and friends gather to watch a movie in the White House screening room. Tonight it's a 3-D sci-fi thriller. Finally a chance to sit down!

Por la noche, la familia y los amigos se reúnen para ver una película en la sala de proyecciones de la Casa Blanca. Hoy ponen un suspenso de ciencia-ficción en 3-D. ¡Al fin una oportunidad de sentarse!

ADVENTURES INTO T[H]E

3D ROBO[T] MONSTER

IN TRU-STEREO
3DIMENSION

MOON MONSTERS LAUNCH ATTACK AGAINST EARTH!

HOW CAN SCIENCE MEET THE MENACE of ASTRAL ASSASSINS! New SCIENCE-FICTION THRILLS!

3D specs

with GEORGE NADER
CLAUDIA BARRETT
Produced by AL ZIMBALIST
RELEASED THRU ASTOR PICTURES CORP

After Sasha and Malia go to bed, President Obama goes back to his office to catch up on his reading. He has stacks of paperwork to go through, but he always spends at least thirty minutes reading just for fun. He enjoys books about his hero, Abraham Lincoln.

Cuando Sasha y Malia se acuestan, el presidente Obama vuelve a su despacho para ponerse al día con todo lo que tiene para leer. Tiene montones de papeles que revisar, pero siempre pasa treinta minutos leyendo algo que le gusta. Le encantan los libros sobre su héroe, Abraham Lincoln.

It's been a long day. After a quick look at his BlackBerry® smart phone, he asks Reggie Love, his personal assistant, to take him to his home upstairs. Mr. Love presses the button, then asks the President one more question: "What's it like to be President Barack Obama?"

Ha sido un día muy largo. Después de echar un vistazo a su Blackberry® Smartphone, le pide a Reggie Love, su asistente personal, que lo conduzca a su casa, en el piso de arriba. El señor Love aprieta el botón, y le hace una pregunta más al Presidente: "¿Qué se siente al ser el presidente Barack Obama?".

THE WHITE HOUSE

LA CASA BLANCA

FURTHER READING/LECTURAS RECOMENDADAS

Works Consulted/Obras consultadas

Fiore, Fay. "Malia and Sasha's Big Move." *Los Angeles Times*, November 18, 2008. http://www.latimes.com/news/politics/la-na-obamafamily18-2008nov18,0,6502045.story

Fox News. "The First 100 Days of the Presidency." http://www.foxnews.com/politics/first100days/index.html

Obama, Barack. *The Audacity of Hope.* New York: Crown Publishers, 2006.

Obama, Barack. *La audacia de la esperanza.* Nueva York: Vintage Español, 2007

Obama, Barack. *Dreams of My Father.* New York: Three Rivers Press, 1995.

Obama, Barack. *Los sueños de mi padre.* Nueva York: Vintage Español, 2009

Thomas, Evans. *A Long Time Coming.* New York: Public Affairs, 2009.

Stolberg, Sheryl Gay. "White House Unbuttons Its Formal Dress Code" *New York Times,* January 29, 2009. http://www.nytimes.com/2009/01/29/us/politics/29whitehouse.html?_r=1

Street, Paul Louis. *Barack Obama and the Future of American Politics.* Boulder, CO: Paradigm Publishers, 2009.

On the Internet

Ben's Guide to the U.S. Government for Kids: The President of the United States
http://bensguide.gpo.gov/9-12/government/national/president.html

The Whitehouse: First Lady Michelle Obama
http://www.whitehouse.gov/administration/michelle_obama/

The Whitehouse: President Barack Obama
http://www.whitehouse.gov/administration/president_obama/

En Internet

Barack Obama en Español
http://my.barackobama.com/page/content/espanol

Whitehouse.gov en Español
http://www.whitehouse.gov/spanish/

INDEX/ÍNDICE